Deleted

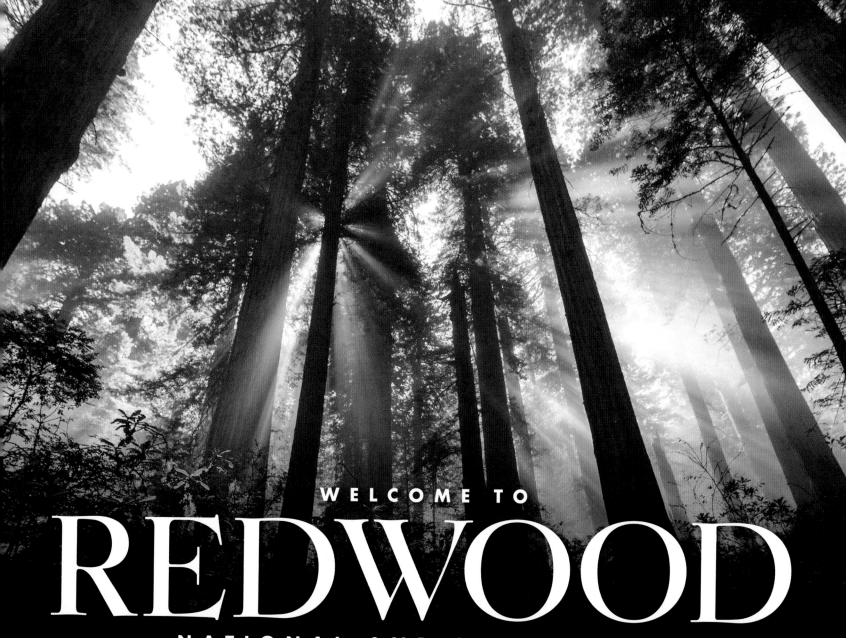

WELCOME TO
REDWOOD
NATIONAL AND STATE PARKS

BY M.J. COSSON

Content Consultants: Jeff Denny and James Wheeler, Redwood National and State Parks

MAP KEY
The maps throughout this book use the following icons:

🏕️ Campground

🚗 Driving Excursion

🥾 Hiking Trail

🔭 Overlook

🪑 Picnic Area

✳️ Point of Interest

🧍 Ranger Station

❓ Visitor Center

🌼 Wildflower Area

🦌 Wildlife Viewing Area

🌲 Wooded Area

About National Parks

A national park is an area of land that has been set aside by Congress. National parks protect nature and history. In most cases, no hunting, grazing, or farming is allowed. The first national park in the United States—and in the world—was Yellowstone National Park. It is located in parts of Wyoming, Idaho, and Montana. It was founded in 1872. In 1916, the U.S. National Park Service began.

Today, the National Park Service manages more than 415 sites. Some of these sites are historic, such as the Statue of Liberty or the Martin Luther King Jr. National Historic Site. Other park areas preserve wild land. The National Park Service manages 40% of the nation's wilderness areas, including national parks. Each year, millions of people from around the world visit these national parks. Visitors may camp, go canoeing, or go for a hike. Or, they may simply sit and enjoy the scenery, wildlife, and the quiet of the land.

TABLE OF

The Child's World®
childsworld.com

Published by The Child's World®
1980 Lookout Drive
Mankato, MN 56003-1705
800-599-READ • www.childsworld.com

ISBN
9781503823457

LCCN
2017944752

Cartographer
Matt Kania/Map Hero, Inc.

Photo Credits
Aleksei Potov/Shutterstock.com: 26; barry maas/Shutterstock.
com: 19 (right); Frank Fennema/Shutterstock.com: 8-9;
HadelProductions/iStockphoto.com: 15, 21; Ian Dagnall/Alamy
Stock Photo: 19 (left); James Mattil/Shutterstock.com: 7; John A.
Anderson/Shutterstock.com: 13, 16-17; Lehakok/Dreamstime:
16 (left); Michael Nichols/Getty: 6-7; Pgiam/iStockphoto.com:
20; randy andy/Shutterstock.com: 23; Savageslc/iStockphoto.
com: 1; shinnji/Shutterstock.com: 12; Tim Zurowski/Shutterstock.

On the cover and this page
The redwoods in Lady Bird Johnson Grove
can seem mysterious.

On page 1
Redwoods stretch toward the early morning
sun in Del Norte Coast Redwoods State Park.

On pages 2–3
Beautiful ocean views can be seen from many
areas of the park.

WELCOME TO REDWOOD NATIONAL AND STATE PARKS

▲

CONTENTS

🚶🚶

Old-Growth Forests

Welcome to Redwood National and State Parks! Look up, and you'll see the tallest trees on Earth. Many are more than 350 feet (107 m) tall.

Can you believe the seeds of these huge trees are the size of a tomato seed? However, not many big redwood trees grew from a seed. The tall trees have been growing for hundreds of years. Some are more than a thousand years old! We call these forests full of old, tall trees "old-growth" forests. There aren't many old-growth forests left.

Redwood National and State Parks

CALIFORNIA

Redwood Clones

Redwood trees have **burls** full of buds that can make more trees. Sometimes you'll see a ring of trees that have grown from a stump. Sometimes you'll see a row that has grown from a fallen tree. Most redwood trees are **clones** from older trees.

Losing the Redwoods

Two hundred years ago, there were 2 million acres (809,371 hectares) of old-growth redwood forest. Now there are 80,000 acres (32,375 hectares). About half of it is within Redwood National and State Parks. Logging of redwoods began in 1850, during the California gold rush. Because the wood is so sturdy and valuable, most redwood forests not within parks are still being **logged** today.

Redwoods grow up to 30 miles (48 km) inland. They rise along the Pacific coast, from the middle of California to southern Oregon. Redwoods need perfect growing conditions. Temperatures must be between 40 and 80 degrees F (4–27 C). Other plants, such as Sitka spruce, protect them from the ocean's salt spray. They depend on steady winter rains and summer fog for moisture. The roots of these trees only grow about 12 feet (4 m) deep, but they spread out for 60 to 80 feet (18–24 m).

People of the Redwood Forest

B egin your visit at the Thomas H. Kuchel Visitor Center, found at the south end of the park. A redwood lumber mill once stood here. You'll learn about the prairie, river, coastline, and forest **habitats** that make up Redwood National and State Parks.

You may see the Yurok Indians performing a demonstration of their traditional brush dance. Native American people have lived in this area for thousands of years. The gold rush brought American settlers and prospectors who pushed them off the lands they had lived on for centuries. Today, many Native Americans still live near the parks.

The Native Americans did not cut down redwood trees. They made dugout canoes and homes from fallen redwood. They thought of each house as a living being with a spirit. They dug a pit and built walls around it from redwood **planks**. The level ground between the pit and the walls was used for storing things.

A Yurok fisherman paddles a dugout canoe in 1923.

Three Types

Earth's air was once quite moist. Redwood-type trees grew everywhere until the last ice age. Three types have **evolved**:

- California's coastal redwood is tallest.
- California's sequoia, from the western side of the Sierra Nevada Mountains, is biggest around.
- The dawn redwood, which is originally from a valley in China, is smallest.

The Spanish were the first Europeans to see redwood trees. Jedediah Smith was the first American person known to explore this area well. From 1826 to 1828, he explored from the Great Salt Lake to the coast. You'll notice the name *Smith* on several features in the park.

Dawn redwoods like this one are often planted in yards and city parks because they grow quickly. These trees are also popular because their leaves turn a beautiful reddish-yellow color in the fall.

Tall coastal redwoods reach toward the sky in Jedediah Smith Redwoods State Park. This park makes up the northernmost part of Redwood National and State Parks, and is a favorite area with campers and hikers.

Forest Stories

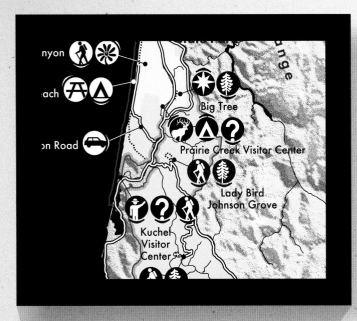

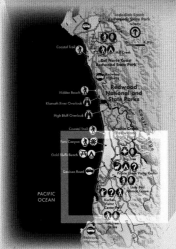

At the Lady Bird Johnson **Grove**, you can see the many layers, or stories, of the redwood forest. The upper story, called the **canopy**, contains the tops of the tallest trees. Redwoods are tallest, but there are also Douglas fir, Sitka spruce, and western hemlock. The middle story has tanoak, madrone, red alder, and vine maple.

The ground cover includes berry bushes, sword ferns, redwood sorrels, redwood violets, mosses, mushrooms, and rhododendron. Fallen trees slowly rot. They serve as a nursery in which new plants grow.

Several hundred black bears roam the park, but you probably won't see any. Chances are, a bear will run away if it sees you first! Park rangers remind you to be "bear aware." Don't leave food or garbage out. If you see a bear on a trail, don't run. Hike in groups and make a lot of noise.

🚶🚶 Rhododendrons bloom along one of the park's many trails. Rhododendrons in coastal forests have pink flowers.

Goose Pens

Because of the moisture, fire is rare in the redwood forest. Sometimes ground cover will burn and clean the forest floor. Redwoods don't burn easily. The bark on a redwood can be 1 foot (30 cm) thick. Fire can scar a redwood, however. The resulting hollow area is called a "goose pen," because in the past, settlers kept chickens and geese there.

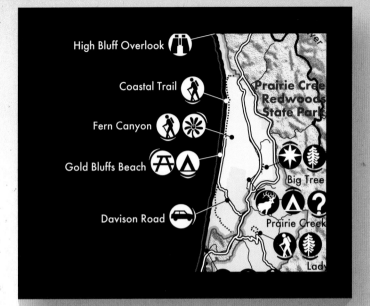

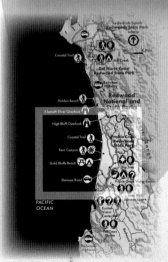

Take Davison Road to Gold Bluffs Beach, along the coast. Go through Fern Canyon. You have probably noticed the ferns that cover the ground in the forests. Here, the 30-foot (9-m) canyon walls are covered in ferns.

The wet, shady conditions in Fern Canyon are perfect for growing ferns. Mosses and other moisture-loving plants can also be found here.

From Prairie to Big Tree

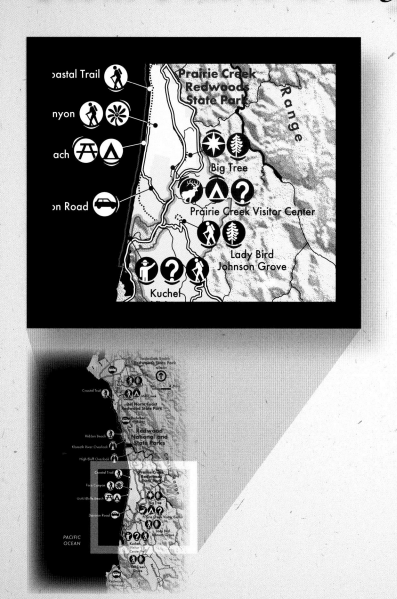

Now you're in Prairie Creek Redwoods State Park. Look for Roosevelt elk on the prairie, but don't go near them. They look peaceful as they graze, but elk are wild animals. Their **grazing** helps keep the prairie free of trees.

Look for black-tailed deer, coyotes, and foxes. Mountain lions and bobcats like the prairie, too, but they usually hunt at night. The prairie is good hunting ground for **raptors** such as the kestrel, the red-tailed hawk, or the great horned owl. They are looking for gophers and meadow mice.

Your next stop is Big Tree. This approximately 1,500-year-old tree is 286 feet (87 m) tall and 74.5 feet (23 m) around. This is not even the biggest tree! Redwood trees are about 370 feet (113 m) tall. That's taller than a 30-story skyscraper!

🚶🚶 Big Tree is huge—and a few of the trees in the park are even bigger!

🚶🚶 Roosevelt elk are also known as Olympic elk. They are the largest type of elk, standing over 5 feet (1.5 m) at the shoulder and weighing 900 pounds (408 kg) or more. Roosevelt elk are darker in color than other elks, and they eat a diet of grasses and berries.

Parts of the old Redwood Highway can seem like a long tunnel through the giant trees.

The road you are taking is part of the old Redwood Highway. This roadway was cleared in the early 1900s. That made it possible for lumber companies to log. It also allowed people to see the grand redwoods up close. A 90-year-old postcard shows the same scene you see today.

Saving the Redwoods

Since the late 1800s, people have worked to save the redwoods. In 1918, the Save the Redwoods League (SRL) was founded. SRL buys land for parks. Over the years, SRL has protected more than 165,000 acres (66,773 hectares) of redwood forests. SRL has saved more than half of the redwood acres in state parks.

Some of the park's prettiest views can be seen by driving sections of the old Redwood Highway.

The Coastal Trail

Now go north to High Bluff Overlook to view the ocean. In spring and fall, you can see gray whales **migrating**. First you may see a spout of water. Soon a whale might surface for a breath of air. You'll also see gulls, ospreys, and cormorants. Sea lions play in the water or nap on the beach or rocks.

On the north side of Klamath River, near the mouth, you come to Klamath River Overlook. You have a great view of the Pacific coast from here. Turn around to look all the way up the Klamath River valley to the mountains. From here, hike north along the Coastal Trail. At many places along the trail, you'll be able to see the ocean.

Take the short side path to Hidden Beach. At low tide, be sure to look in tide pools for barnacles, sea urchins, limpets, sea stars, sea anemones, and hermit crabs. Enjoy the beach, but don't swim! The **undertow** is very dangerous along this part of the coastline.

The Yurok Loop area is along the Coastal Trail. This 70-mile (113-km) trail winds its way through almost the entire length of the park and is popular with hikers.

The North End

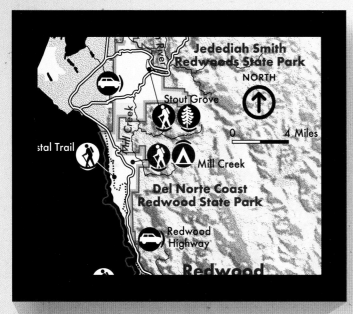

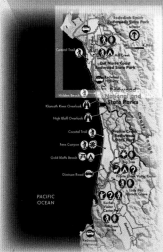

S mith River and Mill Creek are in Jedediah Smith Redwoods State Park. You might see sleek river otters playing in the crystal water. In the fall or winter, you'll see steelhead trout and king salmon in coastal rivers. Salmon are born in rivers or creeks, but live most of their lives in the ocean. They swim back from the ocean, up into the same rivers and creeks in which they were born to **spawn**.

The marbled murrelet (seen below) is an endangered sea bird. It is about the size of a robin. It nests high in very big, old trees. It spends its entire day on the ocean fishing. To help protect this rare bird, don't leave any trash. It attracts Stellar's jays, crows, and ravens. These animals prey on marbled murrelet eggs and chicks. Also, don't make any loud noises. The marbled murrelet prefers quiet.

A Steller's jay perches in one of the parks' trees. The Steller's jay is a large songbird. It can be up to 12 inches (30 cm) long.

Redwoods are known to live for 2,000 years. The tree's official name (the Latin name of *Sequoia sempivirens*) means "forever living tree."

Take Howland Hill Road, an old miner's supply road, to Stout Grove. Howland Hill Road also was the stagecoach route to Oregon. Stout Grove is an old-growth grove given to the park by the wife of a logging company owner.

As you leave Redwood National and State Parks, think about what Jedediah Smith saw. Think about the homeland of the Yuroks. Today you see just a small part of the vast forests they experienced. Be glad that this land and these last remaining forests have been preserved for future generations to enjoy, too.

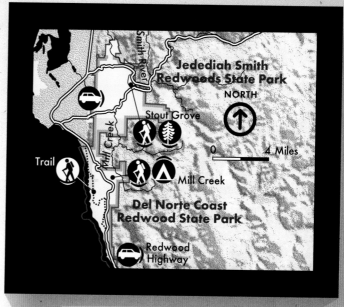

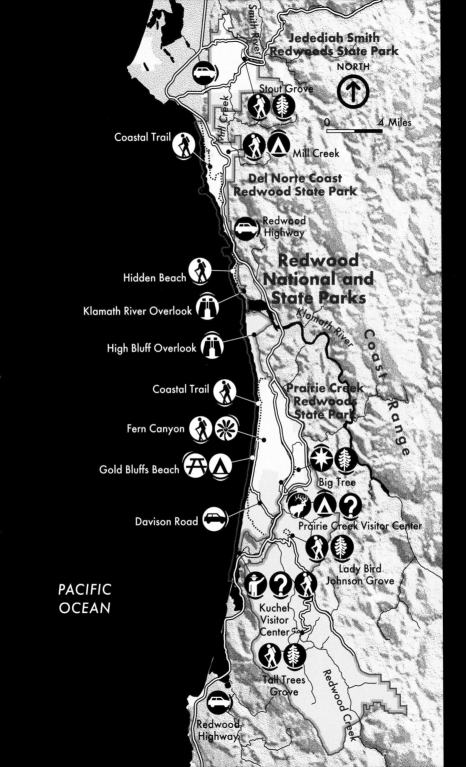

Redwood
National
and State
Parks

CALIFORNIA

Jedediah Smith
Redwoods State Park

NORTH

0   4 Miles

Stout Grove

Coastal Trail

Mill Creek

Del Norte Coast
Redwood State Park

Redwood
Highway

Redwood
National and
State Parks

Hidden Beach

Klamath River Overlook

High Bluff Overlook

Coastal Trail

Prairie Creek
Redwoods
State Park

Fern Canyon

Gold Bluffs Beach

Big Tree

Davison Road

Prairie Creek Visitor Center

Lady Bird
Johnson Grove

Kuchel
Visitor
Center

PACIFIC
OCEAN

Tall Trees
Grove

Redwood
Highway

28

REDWOOD NATIONAL AND STATE PARKS FAST FACTS

Date established: Prairie Creek Redwoods State Park was established August 13, 1923. Del Norte Coast Redwoods State Park was established on October 26, 1925, and Jedediah Smith Redwoods State Park was established on June 3, 1929. Redwood National Park was established on October 2, 1968. The park was expanded on March 27, 1978. Redwood National and State Parks (made up of all four parks) was established in 1994.

Location: Pacific coast of northern California

Size: 206 square miles (534 sq. km); 131,983 acres (53,412 hectares)

Major habitats: Forest, prairie, coastline, and rivers

Elevation:
  Highest: 3,092 feet (942 m) at Schoolhouse Peak
  Lowest: Sea level. The park boundary actually extends ¼ mile out into the ocean so that marine life in the area can be protected under the parks' laws.

Weather:
  Average yearly rainfall: 60–80 inches (152–203 cm)
  Average temperatures: 45–75 F (7–24 C)

Number of animal species: 75 mammal species, 400 bird species, and 15 species of salamander

Number of plant species: 856

Number of endangered or threatened animal/plant species: 11—California brown pelican, tidewater goby, bald eagle, western snowy plover, marbled murrelet, northern spotted owl, coho salmon, Chinook salmon, steelhead trout, Steller's sea lion, and the beach layia

Native people: Chilula, Hupa, Tolowa, and Yurok

Number of visitors each year: About 1 million

Important landforms: Forests, beaches, seastacks, prairie, rivers, streams, and cliffs

Important sites and landmarks: Smith River National Recreation Area, Jedediah Smith Redwoods State Park, Del Norte Coast Redwoods State Park, Prairie Creek Redwoods State Park, and Gold Bluffs Beach

Tourist activities: Camping, hiking, fishing, sightseeing, scenic drives, campfire programs, junior ranger programs, and nature walks

GLOSSARY

burl (BURL): A burl is a knotty growth in a tree containing bud material. In the redwood, a burl is full of buds that can sprout into new trees.

canopy (KAN-uh-pee): The top layer (the tallest trees) in a forest is called its canopy. Redwoods are among the canopy trees in a redwood forest.

clone (KLOHN): A clone is a living thing that comes from another living thing, and is made of the exact same genetic elements as the original. Many redwood trees are clones of older trees.

evolved (eh-VOLVD): Something that has evolved has developed slowly, changing to fill needs. Redwood trees evolved from trees that lived millions of years ago.

grazing (GRAY-zing): Eating grass and green plants from the ground is called grazing. The grazing of Roosevelt elk helps keep trees from taking over the prairies.

grove (GROHV): A group or stand of trees, smaller than a forest, is called a grove. The Stout Grove is a stand of trees in Jedediah Smith Redwoods State Park.

habitat (HAB-uh-tat): A habitat is the type of place in which different plants and animals live. Forests, prairies, the coastline, and rivers are habitats in Redwood National and State Parks.

logged (LOGD): Forests that have been cut down for their wood have been logged. Redwood trees have been logged for more than 150 years.

migrating (MY-grayt-ing): Moving from one habitat to another because of a change in seasons is called migrating. Gray whales are migrating during spring and fall.

planks (PLANKS): Pieces of wood that have been cut into long, flat, and narrow rectangular pieces are planks. A lumber mill saws redwood into planks.

raptors (RAP-turz): Birds of prey—birds that eat smaller birds and small mammals—are raptors. Kestrels and owls are raptors.

spawn (SPAWN): To spawn is to produce and lay eggs. Steelhead trout swim upstream to spawn.

undertow (UN-der-toh): The pull of water away from the shore and toward the sea after a wave has broken onshore is called the undertow. It is dangerous to swim along the coastline because of the undertow.

TO FIND OUT MORE

Λ

FURTHER READING

Bullard, Lisa.
The Redwood Forests.
Minneapolis, MN: Lerner Publications, 2010.

Chin, Jason.
Redwoods.
New York, NY: Roaring Brook Press, 2009.

Halter, Loretta.
A Voice for the Redwoods.
Boulder Creek, CA: Nature's Hopes & Heroes, 2008.

Kras, Sara Louise.
Redwood.
Logan, IA: Perfection Learning, 2003.

ON THE WEB

Visit our home page for lots of links about
Redwood National and State Parks:

childsworld.com/links

NOTE TO PARENTS, TEACHERS, AND LIBRARIANS:
*We routinely check our Web links to make sure they're safe, active sites—
so encourage your readers to check them out!*

INDEX